CW00548456

ZWINGLI
&
CALVIN

by

JOHN BROOME

GOSPEL STANDARD PUBLICATIONS
1991

7 Brackendale Grove, Harpenden, Herts.,
AL5 3EL, England

ULRIC ZWINGLI

ZWINGLI was born in the village of Wildhaus in the valley of Toggenburg in South-East Switzerland on New Year's Day 1484. His father was a shepherd—his home a cottage on the mountain-side. He was one of eight boys. He spent his early years in the mountain valley, until at the age of nine he went to school at Wesen and later to a school at Basle. In these early years he showed signs of brilliance. His father decided to send him to the most famous school in Switzerland at Berne. Here he studied Latin and Greek under one of the most brilliant teachers in Switzerland. But he came in danger of being persuaded to enter a Dominican monastery, and when his father heard of it, he ordered him to return home to Wildhaus. While his father had connections with the Church—he had a brother who was Dean of Wesen and had advised him on young Ulric's education—he had no intention of letting his son become a monk. Wylie comments on this, "The hand that led Luther into the convent, guided Zwingli past it." Though he went home at the command of his father, Zwingli had now become a scholar and felt unable to rest in the shepherd's life of his family. So on the advice of his uncle, he went to Vienna and entered the High School there to resume his studies in Classics and also take up Philosophy. He stayed in Vienna from 1500-1502 and then again returned to Wildhaus. Now eighteen, he returned for a second time to Basle to teach in a school there and study at the University. He received his Master of Arts degree at Basle, but he never made use of it in his life, saying that, "One is our Master, even Christ."

Between 1512-1516 there came to Switzerland a number of men afterwards to be distinguished in the Reformation. Leo Juda, a little man with a sickly body, but a fearless spirit, formed a friendship with Zwingli at Basle which lasted to their death. Both men were later to work in conjunction in the work of the defence of the Gospel. Another whose eyes the work of the defence of the Gospel. Another whose eyes were being opened was Wolfgang Capito, who had been born in Germany in 1478 and came to Basle in 1512. He had started to study the Epistle to the Romans and it had so opened his eyes to the errors of the Roman Catholic Church, that though a priest he soon found it against his conscience to perform the Mass. John Hausschein—called in Greek Oecolampadius (light of the house), a close friend of Capito, came to Basle in 1515, at the invitation of the Bishop, to preach in the city. All these men, including Zwingli were at the time loyal members of the Roman Catholic Church, the only Church in Europe, but while remaining in it their eyes were gradually being opened to its heresies. In this period Erasmus the famous Greek scholar came to Basle. He had just translated the New Testament into Latin from the original Greek and published it at Basle on 1st Feb. 1516; Oecolampadius had helped him in the work. Another man of repute was Thomas Wittenbach. He had come to Basle in 1505 and it was at his lectures that Zwingli first met his life-long friend Leo Juda. It was Wittenbach who, skilled in Hebrew, Greek and Latin, had studied the Scriptures in their original languages and had come to a knowledge of the glorious Gospel. He was the first to show Zwingli and others that beside the scholastic theology of the Roman Catholic Church founded on the teaching of Thomas Aquinas, there was a Biblical doctrine from which that Church had wandered—a far older doctrine—the death of Christ as the only ransom for our souls. Here was the seed of the Gospel, first sown in the heart of Zwingli under the power of the Holy Spirit, through the teaching of Wittenbach. Such men as we have mentioned in this group at Basle who influenced the young Zwingli, were the morning stars of the Reformation in Switzerland. Many greater names have succeeded them. Wylie expresses it very well when he says, "Be the world's day ever so long or ever so bright, the stars that shone in the dawn (of the Reformation) will never cease to shine." The lives of the saints are to the glory and praise of God and all glory redounds to His Name as we remember these men taught of the Spirit in such a dark and erroneous era of the Church's history. Let us beware of returning to the same darkness and error again.

In 1506 another step in Zwingli's career opened for him. He was invited to become pastor of the parish of Glarus. He was ordained a clergyman at Constance and took up his post shortly afterwards at the age of twenty-two. His parish was a very large one, embracing nearly one third of a Canton. He had a serious concern for the spiritual welfare of his flock, though he still spent much of his time in studying the classics, not wholly devoting himself to the Scriptures. He still had much to learn and much to give up. He founded a Latin School at Glarus and sent his pupils to his old University at Vienna. In this period in his life he was forced to take part in a war which Pope Julius II was waging against France. A Swiss Cardinal led some of the clergy of Switzerland and their parishioners across the Alps to fight on behalf of the Pope in a war from which many did not return. The scenes of carnage and the awful spectacle of a religious war added to Zwingli's doubts about the Roman Catholic Church. When he returned he took up his Greek studies and began to read the New Testament in its original tongue. Wylie says, "The young priest of Glarus now placed himself in the presence of the Word of God." A beautiful scene, after the dark days of Medieval Catholicism with all its mysticism and superstition, for the Holy Spirit to direct a man's thoughts and desires to a study of His Holy Word. And Zwingli more than Luther and the other Reformers was shown so clearly two great principles regarding the Word of God; firstly its sole, infallible authority for all teaching, doctrine and practice in the Church; secondly its own self-interpreting nature, Scripture being expounded by Scripture, and not to be interpreted by any one body of men or scholars such as the Roman Catholic Church claimed and still claims. The Spirit, Zwingli maintained, revealed the meaning of Scripture to every earnest and prayerful reader. He said, "The Scriptures come from God, not from men and even that God who enlightens will give thee to understand that the speech comes from God. The Word of God . . . cannot fail; it is bright, it teaches itself, it discloses itself, it illumines the soul with all salvation and grace, comforts it in God, humbles it so that it loses itself and even forfeits itself, and embraces God in itself." Zwingli had experienced what he wrote about in his own soul. Having come from a dry study of the classics and philosophy to the Scriptures, he found in them light and life.

Writing in 1522 Zwingli says, "When seven or eight years ago, I began to give myself wholly up to the Holy Scriptures, philosophy and theology would always keep suggesting quarrels to me. At last I came to this, that I thought, 'Thou must leave all that is false and learn the meaning of God purely out of His own simple Word.' Then I began to ask God for His light and the Scriptures began to be much easier to me, although I am but lazy." Here we have a view of Zwingli's struggles in coming to an understanding of the Scriptures and the battle of reasoning which preceeded his acceptance of it under the teaching of the Holy Spirit. From neither Wittemburg nor Geneva could he obtain any help in this matter. He had not even heard of Luther at this time in his life and Calvin was still a boy at school. Zwingli learnt the truth alone, just as Luther and Calvin were taught, by a study of the Scriptures under the teaching of the Holy Spirit. He said, "I began to preach the Gospel in the year of grace 1516, at that time namely when even the name of Luther had not been heard in our country." Wolfgang Capito also spoke of this early period in the Reformation, his words being recorded in a letter to Bullinger where he wrote, "Before Luther had appeared in public, Zwingli and I had conversed together regarding the overthrow of the Pope." Here is seen the mighty hand of God working in individual hearts and bringing about the Reformation, each Reformer having his own individual work to do.

The Reformation in Switzerland had a different character about it to that in Germany. Wylie suggests that the differences varied according to the kind of error which each part of the Reformation exposed and attacked. Luther attacked the system of Roman Catholic theology which grounded salvation on works such as penances, indulgences, confessions, absolutions and masses. Luther's answer to this was the doctrine of justification by faith, by which he exposed the monastic ideal of 'a holy life'. Zwingli on the other hand attacked the scholastic type of theology of such men as Aquinas with its philosophical system of rules and laws by which a man might by his free-will and intellect discover the truth and become spiritually illuminated. Zwingli's answer was to emphasise the sole authority of the Word of God, the infallibility of Scripture, removing reason from the supreme place which scholastic theologians had given it. He of all the Reformers had the clearest view of the Gospel based on Scripture alone, and all doctrine and practice deriving from it. He was more clearly shorn of all the trappings of Roman Catholicism than Luther—especially in his view of the Lord's Supper, coming as he did, to the view of the simple service of remembrance.

In 1516 Zwingli was offered the post of Preacher at the monastery of Einsiedeln. This contained one of the most famous shrines in Switzerland to which thousands came every year on pilgrimage to obtain the indulgences secured by a visit to the statue of the Virgin Mary, "Our Lady of Einsiedeln," said to perform miracles. The monastery was near Lake Zurich and the Abbot was strangely a man set on removing superstition from his Abbey. Zwingli was in some doubt whether to accept the offer, as he could see himself being shut away in this mountain retreat just at a time when his heart was set on spreading the Gospel. But on consideration he realised that in such a place he could spread the truth to the thousands of pilgrims who came to Einsiedeln each year. So he accepted the offer and from the shrine of "Our Lady of Einsiedeln" pilgrims heard the Gospel, were warned of the futility of coming to the statue of Our Lady for indulgences and told the way of salvation through Christ and Him crucified. Many rejoiced to hear the Good News, but for some, rather like Naaman, the way Zwingli preached seemed too easy and they preferred the hard tortuous mountain climb and the long pilgrimage to the shrine, seeing in such works of their own their way of salvation. These objected to being told on reaching the monastery the utter futility of their labours. But for others, the Gospel reached their hearts and they went back to their homes with a love for it. So out of this centre of spiritual barrenness came forth meat and the

shrine of "Our Lady of Einsiedeln" became a centre for the
propagation of the Reformed Truth. Gradually the numbers
of the pilgrims lessened as Zwingli's work prospered. The
Pope did not interefere. Zwingli's Bishop was only too well
aware what was going on, but he also knew that Zwingli had
brought his parishioners from Glarus to fight on the Pope's
behalf against the French and as the Pope might still need
this help in future he saw no need to antagonise Zwingli.

Zwingli continued his work at Einsiedeln for three years;
then in December 1518 the post of Preacher at the College of
Canons at Zurich became vacant and on 11th December
Zwingli was elected to the office. The work of the Canons
was to conduct the services of the Cathedral and run the
Cathedral School. So Zwingli had the pulpit of Zurich Cathedral from which to preach the everlasting Gospel. It would
seem that among the Canons were some who had an interest
in the Gospel, for them to have elected Zwingli to the office
of Preacher. Zurich was the central city of the Swiss Cantons.
On 1st January 1519, on his thirty-fifth birthday, Zwingli
preached his first sermon from the pulpit of Zurich Cathedral
—a position which gave him a hearing throughout Switzerland. How remarkable that the Lord should raise up and
place His servant in such a prominent position at such a
time. Not many months previously on 31st October 1517,
Luther had posted his 95 Theses on the door of the Castle
Church at Wittemburg. Zwingli began his ministry by reading
the first chapter of the Gospel of Matthew and expounding it.
He continued on successive Sundays to go through the same
Gospel. The two leading subjects of his ministry were the
Word of God, the one infallible authority of the Church; and
the death of Christ, a complete sacrifice for sin. He was also
fired with patriotism for his country which caused him to
urge his fellow countrymen to seek to free themselves from
the shackles of the Papacy. He had been a witness of the
Papal wars with France and had been sickened by the sight.

He was to be further sickened in 1518 by the sight of the
sale of indulgences in Switzerland. The same traffic,
authorised by the Pope to Tetzel in Germany was given in
Switzerland to a man called Bernadin Samson, an Italian

monk. He travelled through Switzerland offering his indulgences for sale. When he came to Zurich, Zwingli prevailed on the City councillors to refuse him entrance, and although they later let him in, as he pretended to have a special message for them from the Pope, they refused to allow him to sell any of his indulgences. Zwingli told the inhabitants of Zurich "God only can forgive sins; none on earth can pardon sin. You may buy this man's papers but be assured you are not absolved. He who sells indulgences is a sorcerer like Simon Magus; a false prophet like Balaam; an ambassador of the king of the bottomless pit." Shortly after this visit of Samson to Switzerland, the country was struck by the plague, "the Great Death", and this showed the awful fallacy of resting one's hope on Papal indulgences. Death swept across the country in the Autumn of 1519 and hourly Zwingli was at the bedside of dying members of his congregation. Eventually he went down with the disease himself and nearly died. In the illness he was firmly persuaded of the truth he had been preaching, being made willing to die and rest his soul's salvation on the Lord Jesus and faith in His finished work on Calvary. It seemed inevitable that like so many others he would die, and news was circulated to that effect. But the Lord spared him to continue the work of the Reformation in Switzerland.

Returning to his pulpit after his illness and the awful effects of the plague, which had left a solemn impression on the hearts of his hearers, Zwingli's ministry took on a deeper vein. He now preached the Law and the Gospel—"As in Adam all die, even so in Christ shall all be made alive." The Cathedral became crowded with hearers. He still remained a Roman Catholic, saying Mass and abstaining from meat on fast days. He did not attempt to overthrow Roman Catholicism, but his aim and object was to restore Christianity to its state as he read of it in the days of the Apostles. He started a Friday lecture for peasants who came to market on that day. On Sundays, having finished preaching on the Gospel of Matthew, he went on to the Acts of the Apostles, the Epistles of Paul and Peter and finally the Hebrews. In a letter dated 31st Dec. 1519, he reported that, "At Zurich upwards of 2,000 souls have already been so strengthened and nourished by the milk of the Word that they can now bear stronger food and anxiously long for it." And from Zurich there spread around Switzerland the seeds of the Reformation. In Lucerne, Myconius, a friend of Zwingli and a schoolmaster, tried to spread the Gospel among his pupils, but was eventually forced to give up and return to Zurich. At Basle, Capito and Hedio, friends of Zwingli, propagated Reformed Truths at this time, though the city did not formally accept the Reformed faith until 1528. Berthold Haller spread the Reformation from Zurich to Bern. He had been a fellow student of Melanchthon and came to Bern as preacher at the Cathedral in 1520. Following the example of Zwingli, he expounded the Gospels in his pulpit at Bern. After a severe struggle, Haller saw the Canton of Bern accept the Protestant Faith in 1528. The event had been preceded by a conference at Bern in which Roman Catholics and Protestants had publicly stated their case. Delegates had come from other Cantons to listen and took back with them many of the truths of the Reformation to other parts of Switzerland. Thus Zurich and her great Reformer Zwingli could claim in the Lord's hand to have had a great influence in the foundation and spread of the Reformation in Switzerland. Haller facing fierce opposition to the Gospel at Bern kept in constant touch with Zwingli. He would perish one day, he feared, trying to preach the Gospel "by the teeth of these bears." "No," replied Zwingli, "you must tame these bear cubs by the Gospel. You must neither be ashamed nor afraid of them. For whosoever is ashamed of Christ before men, of him will Christ be ashamed before his Father." Encouraged by Zwingli's letters Haller pressed on until he was rewarded in seeing the Canton and city of Bern, the first after Zurich of the Swiss Cantons, pass over to the side of the Reformation.

In Zurich Zwingli worked by gradual means, firstly in 1521 attacking the Roman Catholic use of fasts, especially the abstention from eating meat on Fridays. He saw how necessary it was to work slowly, and gradually opened men's minds to the errors of the Church. The Bishops soon realised that to allow even this matter of fasts to be discussed as unscriptural, could lead to other points of Roman Catholic teaching being questioned. They openly attacked Zwingli, and brought the matter before the governing Council of the Canton of Zurich. Zwingli defended himself, quoting I Timothy 4.3. about "abstaining from meats". The Bishop of Constance called his teaching heretical, and the Bishop of Lausanne threatened excommunication to any who read Zwingli's writings or those of Luther. When these attacks failed to silence him, the Bishop of Constance complained to the Diet (Parliament) of the Swiss Confederation. Zwingli, who could see that persecution might soon start, reacted quickly. He called an Assembly of all sympathetic to Reformed teaching at Einsiedeln in 1522. This Assembly sent a petition to the Diet and the Bishop of the Diocese, asking that the Gospel might be preached freely, and priests should be allowed to marry. A summary of the Reformed faith was included with the Petitions, pointing out that such truths were drawn from Scripture, and would, if spread, encourage good living, and clear the country of many evils. The manifesto was ignored by the Church authorities, but became a banner round which the lovers of the Gospel might rally.

In 1523 Zwingli asked the Council of Zurich to allow the Reformation Truths to be debated in public, and this request was granted, the debate beginning on the 29th January. He had printed Sixty-Seven Articles of the Reformed Faith, which he defended from the Scriptures. The first attacked the Church's claim that Scripture had no authority unless sanctioned by the Church. The others stated that Jesus Christ is our only Teacher and Mediator; that He alone is the Head of believers; that all who are united to Him are members of His body, children of God and members of the Church; that Jesus Christ is the one sovereign and eternal Priest; that the Mass is not a sacrifice; that the Bible permits all men, including ministers of the Gospel to marry; that monasteries should be dissolved; that God alone can pardon sin, and that there is no such place as Purgatory after death. These Articles Zwingli had printed before the debate started. They were the Swiss counterpart of Luther's "95 Theses", though not identical in content. Over 600 attended the Conference, though the representatives of the Reformed side came only from Bern and Schaffhausen. This showed how weak their cause was as yet among the Swiss Cantons. The Reformers sat alone at a table in the middle of the Assembly to defend the cause of the Gospel. As Zwingli spoke in defence of the truth, the parallel with Luther at Worms immediately comes to mind, though the Assembly was a less august one. Zwingli argued with Faber, the Bishop's Deputy, and his fellow Reformers Hoffman of Schaffhausen, and Leo Juda spoke as well. But there was no common ground as the Reformers based all their arguments on the Bible, and the Roman Catholic theologians referred constantly to tradition and Decrees of Church Councils. The meeting showed the great division between the two sides. The Council of Zurich issued its Edict after the debate that all the preachers in the city and Canton of Zurich should teach only those things that could be proved from Scripture. This was a victory for Zwingli's cause, though he had a feeling that he had won it too easily.

He now set about writing a book based on accepted practices of worship in the Roman Catholic Church, her ordinances and ceremonies, to show how unrelated they were to Scripture, and lacking in any Biblical authority. This at once received a wide circulation. In his Bible studies on the Acts of the Apostles, he showed the development of the early Christian Church, and the spread of the Gospel, and set about bringing out a practical application in Zurich. The large number of Cathedral Canons were reduced. Payment was abolished for baptism, burial and other rites of the Church; choir services were replaced by preaching and exposition of the Scriptures. The money saved from these reforms was used to found a school in Zurich, train pastors and generally educate the youth of the city. Next he suggested the dissolution of nunneries and monasteries, and the Council of Zurich agreed to this. Nuns had been allowed to leave their cloisters if they wished in 1523, and return to civil society. Some had done so, but others had remained in their cloisters. Now in 1524, the Council officially dissolved the remaining monasteries and nunneries in the city. All the money from the dissolution was devoted to poor relief, benefit for the sick and for education. Then the Council decreed that priests could marry if they so wished. Leo Juda was married shortly after this decree, and Zwingli, who had already been privately married in 1522, celebrated his marriage publicly in the Cathedral Church in April 1524. His marriage had been no secret to his friends or enemies. Its public proclamation marked a further stage in the Swiss Reformation; the denial of the Roman Catholic teaching of a celibate clergy. Thus the Reformation advanced a step at a time and it is remarkable that it did this at Zurich with so little disturbance.

The next step was to abolish the Mass and to clear the Churches of all images. Zwingli first preached on the subject, and afterwards put his ideas down in the form of Eighteen Propositions. Then in October 1523, the Council of Zurich organised another public debate to discuss the two issues of images and the Mass. Nine hundred came to the debate, including 350 priests. Zwingli and Leo Juda sat at the table in the centre of the Assembly to defend the Eighteen Propositions. Zwingli first stated his views on the Church, "that she was created by the word of God, had Christ as her only Head and that the source of all her teaching and authority was the Bible". This was an entirely new view of the Church to most of his hearers, who saw the Church as the organisation which had the Pope as its head. Without such a view, the Assembly before which Zwingli was expressing his views, must have been purely a body of "heretics", those breaking away from the orthodox Roman Catholic teaching. But as Zwingli and his fellow Reformers saw it, it was the Roman Catholic Church who had broken from orthodox Catholic teaching many centuries before, when such concepts as the Mass had been introduced—and they, the Reformers, were merely restoring sound doctrine and teaching according to the Bible. Zwingli claimed an authority to examine the truth in the light of Scripture for the Church of God at Zurich, free from any authority of any other body such as the Roman Catholic Church. Such a concept of the authority of the local Church, he saw as Scriptural, so long as the local Church conformed to the teaching of Scripture. Then from Scripture, he went on to show that all images and the worshipping of them was forbidden, and the Conference accepted this as true. The subject of the Mass was then debated, and Zwingli showed how the Lord's Supper was a memorial and not a sacrifice. "He considered the Supper to be a remembrance instituted by Christ at which He will be present, and whereby He, by means of His word of promise and outward signs, will make the blessing of His death, whose inward power is eternal, to be actually effective in the Christian for the strengthening and assurance of faith," (Dorner, "History of Protestant Theology"). Thus he attacked the material concept of transubstantiation, and any view which approached to it, such as consubstantiation, which suggested the spiritual presence of Christ in the bread and wine rather than His corporeal presence taught in transubstantiation. With hardly one expression of disapproval, the Conference accepted Zwingli's view of the Lord's Supper. This was in fact a far purer view than that of Luther, who still had a mystical view of the words, "This is my body", though he denied transubstantiation. Zwingli moved with caution and did not immediately demand the removal of all images and the abolition of the Mass in Zurich. But images were to be covered over, and those who wished, could receive the Lord's Supper in the articles of bread and wine. The city Council also abolished ritualistic processions in the streets, carrying the Host or wafer, which was a practice of the Roman Catholic Church.

Finally, in June, 1524, the city Council had all images removed from the Zurich Churches. This caused the Diet of the Swiss Confederation to react and threaten to stop the Reformation in Zurich by force, if it were allowed to continue any longer. Switzerland was dividing strongly into Roman Catholic and Protestant areas, and soon civil war would ensue, much against the wish of the Reformers. Before the year 1524 was out, persecution had started, and two supporters of the Protestant Faith were beheaded. Zwingli, far from being frightened at the prospect of a martyr's death, pressed on with his demands for the abolition of the Mass. This was granted by the city Council in 1525. Zwingli preached from Exodus 12 verse 11 "Ye shall eat it in haste: it *is* the Lord's passover." In a dream the previous night, he had been shown how the text, "It *is* the Lord's passover" was so closely parallel to, "This *is* my body," and as he was quite clear that the passover lamb was only a symbol, so he was confirmed in his belief that the bread used in the Lord's Supper was also only a symbol. And so on the Thursday before Easter 1525, the Lord's Supper was celebrated for the first time at Zurich according to the Protestant form. A table was set with a white cloth with wooden plates and bread on them, and wooden goblets filled with wine. The altars were converted into pulpits from which the Gospel was preached before the Lord's Supper was administered. The whole was simply copied from the Last Supper in the upper room as the Lord intended it to be performed. This was one of the key-stones of the Reformation, the Zurich Zwinglian view of the Lord's Supper as a memorial service. Even Luther himself was not brought so far as to see the ordinance in this simple light, and disagreed strongly with Zwingli over the issue. The two met at Marburg in 1529 to discuss their differences of view, but no conclusion was reached and Protestantism was accordingly left divided in Europe over this issue, the Lutheran Church maintaining the doctrine of consubstantiation, and Zwingli and his followers, the simple memorial view of the service. Before they parted, the two sides, Zwinglian and Lutheran, signed the Marburg Confession, in which they stated all the points on which they were agreed, and these included the fundamental core of Protestant truth, the Deity of Christ, original sin and the Fall, justification by faith, the authority of Scripture, and the rejection of tradition. But over the Communion Service there was no agreement.

Within two years of this meeting with Luther, Zwingli had died. The Roman Catholic Cantons of Switzerland had joined up with Roman Catholic Austria to silence the Reformation at Zurich by armed force. The citizens of Zurich prepared to fight, and Zwingli went to battle with them. At first a peace was signed between the Roman Catholics and Protestants, but it was short lived. In September, 1530, the Protestant pastors of Zurich, Bern, Basle and Strasburg met at Zwingli's home in Zurich to discuss the serious situation. A year later, in October, 1531, five Roman Catholic Cantons again prepared for war. The citizens of Zurich, with Zwingli as Chaplain to the Army went out to fight, and were defeated. Zwingli was injured in the battle, was recognised among the wounded and killed in cold blood. Thus on a battle field, the great Reformer met his death. He was no less a martyr for the truth than if he had died at the stake. In Zurich a peace was signed, the only stipulation being for toleration. The Reformed Faith was suppressed, altars were set up, the Mass was restored and monasteries re-opened. Wylie comments; "Zwingli had fallen; but in this same land a mightier was about to arise;" even John Calvin.

JOHN CALVIN

CALVIN was born at Noyon in France in July 1509. His father worked for the local Roman Catholic bishop managing the business affairs of the Cathedral. Educated for a time in Noyon, he went to Paris at the age of fourteen to the College of La Marche, where he received a good grounding in Latin, the international language of Europe at the time, which was to be of such great use to him in his writings for the Reformation—a language which he used for the first and many later editions of his famous work "The Institutes of the Christian Religion." After leaving La Marche he went to the College of Montaigu in 1526. This was a part of Paris University, a training college for Catholic priests. Calvin was a very keen scholar—he rose early to study. At this time the Reformation was well under way—the Diet of Worms had been held in 1521—in 1525 Luther had published "The Bondage of the Will." Calvin was bound to have heard about it. But he came from a strong orthodox Roman Catholic background and it seemed most unlikely that he would be affected by it. But one of his cousins, Olivetan, came to Paris at the time, frequently saw him and had discussions with him about the burning issues of the day. The effect on Calvin was to cause him to have doubts about the Roman Catholic Church which he had always trusted.

It also brought him into conviction of sin. One day he witnessed in Paris the burning of one of the early Protestants and this showed him how great faith these men were given to endure the flames. He asked inwardly the question, how he would die in such circumstances. He then took the advice of his cousin and began to read the Bible. Later in his life in 1557, in his Preface to his "Commentary in the Psalms," he wrote, "I was taken from the study of philosophy and put to learn law from which nevertheless God in His secret providence finally curbed and turned me in another direction. At first, although I was so obstinately given to the superstitions of the Papacy, that it was extremely difficult to drag me from the depths of the mire, yet by a sudden conversion He tamed my heart and made it teachable, this heart which for its age was excessively hardened in such matters." Earlier in a letter written in 1539 he had said, of the Protestants, "There was one thing especially which kept me from believing these people, that was reverence for the Church. But after I had sometimes listened and suffered being taught, I realised that any such fear that the majesty of the Church might be diminished was vain and superfluous. And when my mind had been made ready to be truly attentive, I began to understand as if someone had brought me a light, in what a mire of error I had wallowed and had become filthy and with how much mud and dirt I had been defiled. Being then grievously troubled and distracted, as was my duty on account of the wretched state into which I had fallen, and yet more on account of the knowledge of eternal death which hung over me, I judged nothing more necessary to me after having condemned with groans and tears my past manner of life, than to give myself up and betake myself to Thy way."

Here we have in Calvin's own words how the truth was revealed to him. Like many servants of God, he rarely spoke of God's work in his own soul. Two things stand out—firstly, his obstinacy and secondly how the Lord tamed his spirit and called him suddenly to understand the truth. His deep reverence for the Roman Catholic Church was similar to Luther's. Now he turned his mind from a career in the Church, which he had been pursuing in Paris, and went to Orleans University to study law. He was looking for a career in the world. He moved on to Bourges, still following his studies in law. There he learnt Greek, which was to equip him later in life to understand the New Testament in its original language. Bourges was a favoured city. It was situated in the Province of Berry, whose ruler, Margaret, Queen of Navarre and Duchess of Berry, sympathised with the Reformation cause. Here was a safe seed-ground for the truth and here for some time before Calvin arrived, it had been preached by certain Roman Catholic priests who had come to a knowledge of it. Calvin's views were already known in Bourges before his arrival, and when he came the Protestants asked him to become their leader. He did not agree for some time to preach, because he had such a clear view of the greatness of the work and his unfitness to undertake it. But it is said that here at Bourges in 1529, Calvin started preaching and various places are shown in the area today, where he is said to have preached in the open air, in market-places and the surrounding villages. He was twenty years of age at the time.

In 1531 he returned to Noyon for a time, as his father lay dying. After a two-month illness he passed away and Calvin now felt free to give up his career as a lawyer and turn to the Scriptures. He went back to Paris. Here he became friendly with the Rector of the University, Nicolas Cop, for whom he composed a sermon, which the Rector preached in a Paris church on All-Saints Day, 1st November, 1533. The result was that this sermon, which was very evangelical in its content, was denounced by the Franciscan Friars and condemned by the Parlement of Paris. Cop fled from Paris to Basle in Switzerland to escape persecution. Calvin also left Paris quickly and went to Angoulême, near Bordeaux, since the rumour had spread that he was the author of the sermon or had advised Cop on the truth contained in it.

In Angoulême, the birthplace of Margaret of Navarre, he stayed at the home of the Du Tillets, a noble and wealthy family with whom he had been acquainted in Paris. The library of their château contained one of the finest collections of books in France, about 4,000 volumes. Here Calvin did not waste his time. He planned what D'Aubigne has called "the finest work of the Reformation," his book "The Institutes of the Christian Religion." He did not write it at Angoulême, but he collected the materials and arranged the plan of it. Here too he was under the protection of Margaret of Angoulême, Queen of Navarre. He wrote of his escape and place of rest, saying, "When I feared that my stay would be a frightful one, a rest had been prepared for me in quietness, contrary to all expectation and it is the hand of God that has done all this. If we trust Him, He will watch over us Himself." Around him at Angoulême gathered a circle of friends who loved the truth as he did and to them he explained his plans for "The Institutes". He spent a few weeks in Nérac, April-May 1534, a town where Evangelicals met under the protection of the Queen of Navarre (she was sister of the King of France, Francis I). In the same year he also visited Noyon and Paris and then went to Poitiers, where a group of Protestants gathered round him and he discussed the Reformed view of the Lord's Supper as opposed to the Mass, and here the first reformed Lord's Supper was held by the Protestants in secret in a cave. Towards the end of year 1534, Calvin and his friend, Louis Du Tillet, began to feel that they were in danger so long as they remained in France, and so for safety they went first to Strasbourg and finally to Basle in Switzerland.

At Basle Calvin was especially occupied with writing "The Institutes." He was spurred to publish it by events in France following his departure. In Paris on 17th October, 1534 placards had been put up in prominent places by the Protestants condemning the Mass. This angered Francis I, who felt he ought to have a day of national repentance for such heresy. This he did by going in solemn penitent procession to the Cathedral Church of Nôtre Dame to High Mass and on the way back stopping to witness the burning of several Protestant martyrs, among which were some who had been friends of Calvin. Calvin felt he must defend the cause of his dying friends and justify their innocence to the nations of Europe and fully state the cause for which they had died. He says in the first edition of "The Institutes" published in 1536 that "it was a little booklet containing in summary the principal matters, and it had no other object but that people should be informed what faith was held by those whom I could see evil and lawless flatterers were villifying in a foul and most mischievous way." The false accusations concerned sedition and treason, which was the charge levied against the Protestant martyrs in Paris. Calvin set out to show that they died for their belief in justification by faith—the Reformation doctrine. The little book was first published in Latin. Calvin revised and extended it all his life, publishing it in many editions, until it became a large manual of

Reformation teaching and was translated into many languages.

Recently the Soverign Grace Union have issued a summary of it in a paperback. This is the work of J. P. Wiles and is entitled "Instruction in Christianity". It is about 200 pages in length and is more what we imagine Calvin intended it to be when he first published it in 1536. Readers are recommended to obtain a copy from the S.G.U. and read in an easy form the great truths that Calvin laboured to present to the world in 1536 in the face of the burning of his friends at the stake in Paris. Such truths were indelibly written in the hearts of the men who died courageously for them.

During this year Calvin left Basle, shortly after the publication of his "Institutes", and visited Italy, and then returned to Paris. There he settled his business affairs, sold his family estate at Noyon and set out to leave his homeland for ever. Making for Strasbourg, he was forced to change his route because of warfare on the road and so turned to enter Switzerland through Lyons and Geneva. He intended to stay in Geneva one night—but there in that visit he met Farel, who urged him with great vehemence to stay and help him in the Gospel cause and not to seek some quiet corner to study. Calvin speaks of his unwillingness to listen to Farel, the great Swiss Reformer, saying "Yet I remained in my shame and timidity, unwilling to have to take any definite responsibility." Farel, hearing that Calvin wanted to do some study, went so far as to ask, "that it might please God to curse my rest and the tranquillity for study that I was seeking, if in so great a necessity I were to withdraw and refuse to give my help and assistance." Calvin, frightened by this, but still not very willing, agreed to stay, and so began that long association of the great Reformer with the city of Geneva of which Calvin said, "as if God from on high had stretched out His hand to stay me." His night's stay became a life-time and what he had not seen at once to be the Lord's hand proved to be His ordaining.

William Farel, who was twenty years his senior, was also a French exile. The latter had been called by grace about

1521. He says in his book, "The True Face of the Cross,"
"I was so soiled with mire and Papal filth and so deeply
ruined in it, that all that is in heaven and on earth could not
have dragged me from it, if this loving God and this kindly
Saviour Jesus Christ in His great grace had not pulled me
out, drawing me with His Gospel." Later he wrote, "But
when God . . . made Himself known to me through a pious
brother (Lefèvre) as God who will be loved and venerated
alone . . . then my mind was led to Him by various circumstances and having come into port was fixed on Him alone."
Soon after this he was forced to leave France and took refuge
in Switzerland where in 1524 he openly preached the Gospel
for the first time. At Neuchâtel his preaching roused the
people to remove all the statues from the churches. He came
to Geneva to preach in 1532. Violence was raised against
him by the Roman Catholic clergy. He was almost thrown
into the Rhône and had to leave Geneva for a time. Some of
his followers stayed and preached the Gospel in the open air
and after the Gospel obtained a footing, in 1533 Farel was
able to return. In March 1534 he took over a Franciscan
Monastery and used it as a centre from which to spread the
truth. In that year the people of Geneva demolished several
suburbs of the city outside the city walls as a defence against
Roman Catholic princes. In 1536 the attack came in the form
of a siege from the Duke of Savoy. It was relieved by an army
sent by the Protestant city of Berne and the Duke of Savoy
was completely defeated, being forced to retreat, and never
attack Geneva again. In May 1536 the City Council of
Geneva solemnly declared their intention to follow the
Reformed Faith. Two months later Calvin arrived at Geneva
seeking a quiet place of exile and not intending to stay. He
says of the state of the City at the time that "everything was in
confusion."

How urgent then was the situation to Farel. Here was the
young writer of the "Christian Institutes", (Calvin was about
twenty-seven at the time) come to the City at the hour of
crisis. Farel had been able by God's help to stir up the people
against Roman Catholicism. It needed a greater man to lay
the foundation of the new Church. Farel was humble enough

to realise that Calvin was the leader sent as a great teacher for the new Church. Calvin started in a humble way as "lecturer in Holy Scripture". His first important task was to draw up the articles of religion for the Protestant Church. This he did in the form of Twenty-One Articles. Then there developed a dispute between the Ministers of the Reformed Faith and the City Councillors of Geneva. According to the Articles, a man might become a member of the new Church upon a profession of belief in them. They included the right of the Minister to refuse the Lord's Supper to any he considered unfit and men were appointed from the congregation to watch the behaviour of those in the city and report anything which would unfit a man to attend the Lord's Supper. All the people had originally attended the Mass after Confession. Now when the city suddenly became Protestant, it did not necessarily mean all were called by grace, and it rested with the Ministers to watch the Lord's Table, as it was upon a profession of faith and not a confession of experience that membership was granted. But this angered the City Councillors, who ordered the Ministers to give up their right to excommunicate and withhold participation at the Lord's Supper. This Calvin, Farel and the other Reformers refused to do, maintaining that they should control Church order and not the City Council. The result was that in April 1538 the conflict came to a head and the Council ordered Farel, Calvin and the other Reformers to leave Geneva within three days.

Calvin first went to Basle where he supervised a new edition of "The Institutes". Then at the request of the Reformer, Martin Bucer, he made his way to Strasbourg. He was now twenty-nine. Bucer, seventeen years older than him, was one of the first generation of Reformers and knew Luther. Here Calvin was able to discuss the problem of participation at the Lord's Supper. The Roman Catholic confessional had been abolished at Strasbourg. Calvin now substituted for it, an interview with the Minister before the service, for each participant, to guard against abuses. Also overseers were appointed to watch the lives of the people. It seems strange that the Reformers should not use the method of confession before the Church members of a personal experience of conversion, but one must realise that they still accepted infant baptism as a symbol of entrance to church membership. Bucer believed in the four ministries, as he called it—Pastors, teachers, elders, and deacons and Calvin followed this when he returned to Geneva. At Strasbourg in 1539 Calvin published his "Commentary on Romans" and also in the same year a small volume of Psalms in French verse together with the music for singing in the Protestant services. While there he married Idelette de Bure. Their marriage did not last many years, as after a long illness she died in 1549. He referred to her as "my excellent life-companion, who if it had been necessary would have faced with me not only exile and poverty, but even death." Calvin lectured in theology at the Protestant Academy but received no salary. He lived in comparative poverty on his inherited estate and the sale of his books. On occasions he travelled to take part in discussions between Protestants and Roman Catholics, visiting Frankfurt in 1539, Worms and Ratisbon in 1541. At Frankfurt he met Melanchthon whose close friend he became, but he never met Luther. Then as the situation grew quieter at Geneva and those who supported Calvin and Farel increased their influence in the city, the Reformers returned, Calvin in September 1541.

On the first Sunday, he entered the pulpit he had previously vacated, and began to expound the Scriptures from the place where he had left off in 1538. Nothing was said, past recriminations were forgotten and the City Councillors accepted the authority of the Ministers over the Church, though they still attended the sessions of the governing Council of the Church and nominated the elders. The discipline of the Church was controlled by the twelve elders and the Ministers who formed a body known as the Consistory. Calvin now took up the main phase of his life's work from 1541-1564 writing, preaching and lecturing. He had to meet with much opposition in Geneva. One group called 'the Libertines' demanded all the usual wordly pleasures. Things such as dancing, theatrical performances and drunkenness were banned by the City Council supported by the Consistory of the Church. Life in Geneva in the Sixteenth Century was very rough. On occasions Calvin was faced with riots in his Church with drawn swords. The same conduct occurred when he put the case for law, order and morality before the City Council. His influence however, was great for the moral welfare of the people of the city, though he has often been accused of acting dictatorially. In fact, he did little more than the laws of our own country do today to stop open evil.

Gradually around him at Geneva gathered a distinguished group of theologians, noted among whom was Theodore Beza, who after 1552 became his right-hand man and eventually his successor when he died. One immense problem with which Calvin had to deal was the denial of the doctrine of the Trinity by a man called Servetus. Servetus was condemned by the City Council of Geneva for heresy and was burnt there in 1553. This action in which Calvin was concerned has drawn on the Reformed cause the sort of condemnation that Oliver Cromwell's action at Drogheda drew on him. We cannot in any way condone Calvin's agreement with the sentence. The trial was just—all the proceedings were fair with a defence and prosecution. Calvin tried to get the execution changed from burning to beheading. But the fact remains that he agreed with the punishment of death for heresy. Calvin's age saw as much danger in errors of doctrine as in crimes such as murder, and an equivalent punishment was meted out for both. "Calvin was wrong to consider that heresy should be punished by .... death, but he was right to think that the denial of the Trinity and the Divinity of Christ were infinitely serious matters." (Jean Cadier, "The Man God Mastered," p.162, I.V.F.).

In his life Calvin produced Commentaries on most of the books of the Bible. They were the results of many lectures he gave at Strasbourg and at Geneva which were taken down and printed in the form of Commentaries. Last century they were reprinted by the Calvin Translation Society and are in print again today. His influence was very great in his day and since. Exiles gathered at Geneva from many countries including England and Scotland, especially in the reign of Queen Mary, and great men such as John Knox listened to Calvin's lectures. Later Knox applied the principles of faith and discipline he had learnt at Geneva in Scotland. In 1559 an Academy was founded in Geneva on a twofold scheme of the equivalent of present day Secondary and University education and students gathered in large numbers especially from France. Calvin also kept up a large correspondence—his works include four thousand letters to his friends, Farel, Bucer, Beza and many other correspondents, including the King of England, the young Protestant Edward VI and the Archbishop of Canterbury, Thomas Cranmer, who eventually died at the stake in the reign of Mary. For much of his life his health was poor, yet he never spared himself for the sake of the Gospel. He died in 1564 at the comparatively early age of fifty-five. Farel, who was over eighty, outlived him for one year, and walked many miles to visit him on his death-bed. He was buried very simply as was his wish and no stone marks his grave, the exact position of which is now unknown.

His teaching we know so well. He emphasised the doctrines of grace and his theology has its own name in "Calvinism". Yet this is unfair to him. His very wish to be buried without pomp and ceremony showed his desire to leave no system of truth named after him. He was the last person, like Luther, to wish his name to be associated with a particular type of Christianity. In his whole life and work he had one sole aim, namely to give all glory to God. He believed that the revelation of truth which he had was the correct one. He emphasised God's sovereignty, but only because he saw that the whole of truth centred around God's revealed will, and that a Christianity which allowed any say to man's so-called free-will was a denial of God's sovereignty in election. This clear teaching in his writings has stood as a defence of the truth in many generations and it is a great encouragement to witness it being revived today. Such a revival in this country and in the United States is a sign which ought to encourage us, for we live in times when such doctrine is despised by the majority, and we greatly need another Reformation.